You feel bad because you're in a vicious circle

The way you feel is affected by things that happen to you. Like the things on the opposite page. Those things are all outside of you. Sometimes, you can change what's happening outside, but often, you can't do much about them.

And when you allow them to affect your mood, the vicious circle kicks in and you feel worse and worse and worse…

Vicious circles spin by affecting five areas of your life.

Turn over to see how it works

Too Much to do
FRIENDS HATE ME
SOMEONE CLOSE IS REALLY ILL
LOST MY JOB
Got Dumped
BEING ILL
ALTERED THINKING
I'M USELESS
I'M ALL ALONE
Got kicked off the team
GOT CRITICISED
FAILED TEST OR EXAM
BEING BULLIED
No-one to talk to

First, an outside event affects you

When something happens, you naturally notice it and think about it. If you forget your sister's birthday, for example, you may think
"I'm useless!"
This is called **Altered Thinking.**

Altered thinking can set off a chain reaction inside you that affects the way you feel and what you do.

When your altered thinking is negative (like "I'm useless"), the vicious circle is triggered and you can end up really down, not getting out of bed and even feeling ill.

Let's see the
Vicious Circle in action

Altered thinking leads to altered feelings

If you think "I'm useless!" you're going to feel pretty low, sad or guilty.

Maybe you feel as if you've let her down, or you might feel guilty because you know you should have been more organised.

So now what happens?

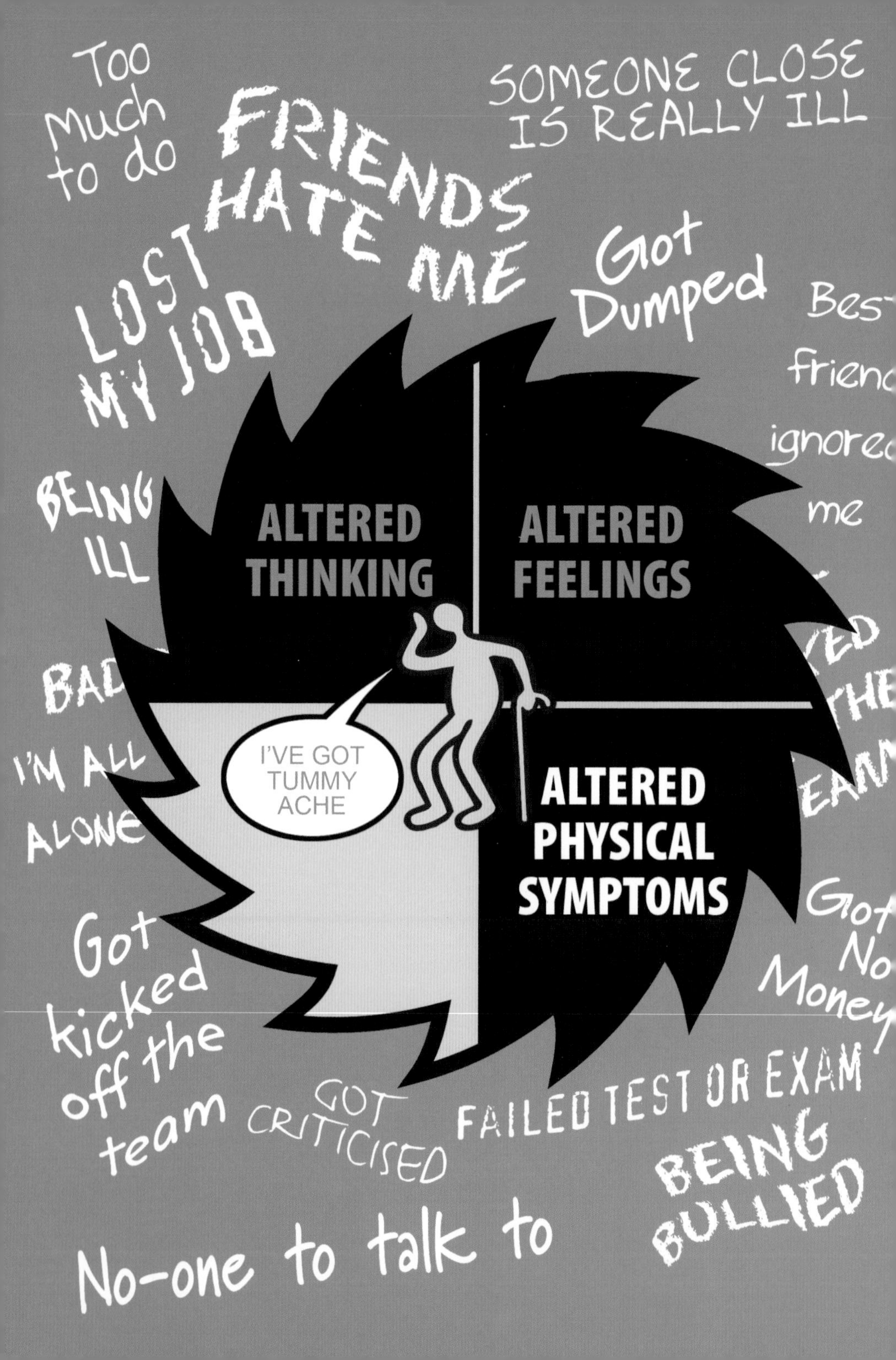

Too much to do
FRIENDS HATE ME
SOMEONE CLOSE IS REALLY ILL
LOST MY JOB
Got Dumped
BEING ILL
ALTERED THINKING
ALTERED FEELINGS
I'VE GOT TUMMY ACHE
ALTERED PHYSICAL SYMPTOMS
I'M ALL ALONE
No Money
Got kicked off the team
GOT CRITICISED
FAILED TEST OR EXAM
BEING BULLIED
No-one to talk to

Altered feelings lead to altered physical symptoms

When you feel low or guilty, you can get sweaty and tense and your stomach or your head can ache. Sometimes you can feel really tired.

Your hands might feel clammy, or you feel really tense and can't sit still.

Ever had a sinking feeling or felt your heart racing? It's probably that old vicious circle spinning round!

What next?

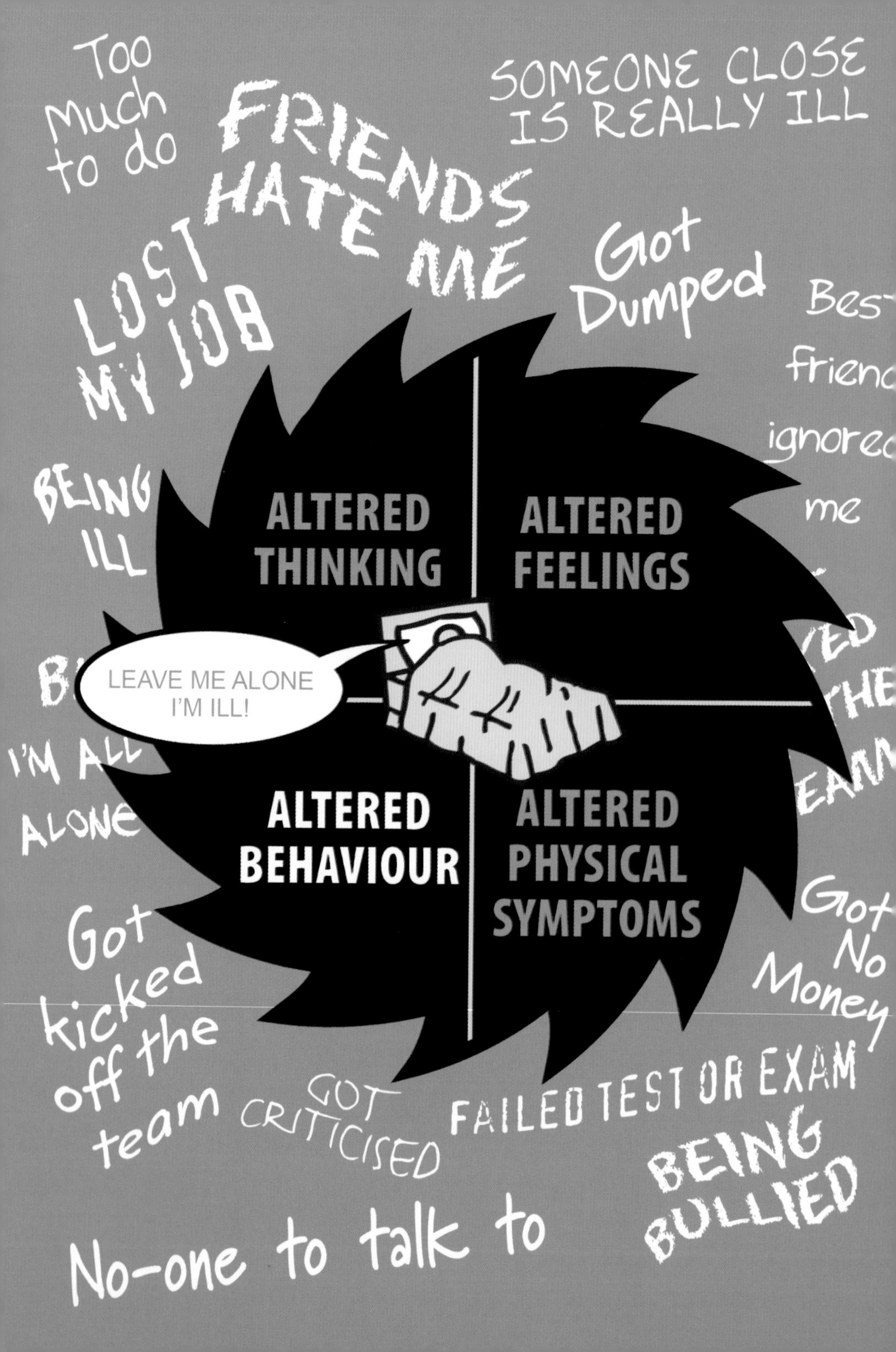

Too Much to do
FRIENDS HATE ME
SOMEONE CLOSE IS REALLY ILL
LOST MY JOB
Got Dumped
BEING ILL
ALTERED THINKING
ALTERED FEELINGS
LEAVE ME ALONE I'M ILL!
I'M ALL ALONE
ALTERED BEHAVIOUR
ALTERED PHYSICAL SYMPTOMS
Got kicked off the team
Got No Money
GOT CRITICISED
FAILED TEST OR EXAM
BEING BULLIED
No-one to talk to

Altered physical symptoms lead to altered behaviour

It's only natural. You're really tired, you have a headache or maybe feel tense, so you don't feel like going out, or even getting up. You steer clear of people who might ask if you sent a card or present. You stay in and hardly do any exercise. You're not eating right and you seem to catch all the bugs that are going round.

You even finish up at the doctor's, asking why you can't seem to shake off this virus you've had for weeks.

And you know what happens then? The circle goes round again, only this time, you're already ill, staying in bed and fed up, so you get even worse.

Vicious, these circles, aren't they? That's why it's important to find out how you feel is affecting these five areas of your life (outside events, thinking, feelings, physical symptoms and behaviour).

Now what about you?

COMPLETE YOUR OWN FIVE AREAS ASSESSMENT

You've read about how you might react if you missed your sisters birthday. Do you fall into other vicious circles from time to time?

Here's how to play detective and work out how the vicious circle affects you.

Choose two recent times when you felt bad. To start with, don't pick times that are really upsetting or distressing. Instead choose situations when you felt a bit down, fed up, angry, stressed, scared, frustrated, guilty, ashamed, tired, or in pain.

Now use the next two pages to work out how you reacted.

Pen at the ready?

Now's time to spot that vicious circle!

People and Events

**Altered
Thinking**

**People and
Events**

**Altered
Behaviour**

ASSESSMENT

People and Events

Altered Feelings

Altered Physical Feelings

People and Events

YOUR
VICIOUS
CIRCLE

Did you fall into a vicious circle?

If you felt bad, it's likely the vicious circle was spinning. What were the outside events like people/difficult situations? Did what you think affect how you felt – in your feelings and physical feelings? How did this affect what you did?

Did anything look familiar? Patterns of thinking, feeling or body reactions often repeat again and again. Did the circle start to spin and make you feel even worse?

Stopping your circle spinning takes practise. If you're feeling worse than usual it can feel hard to break the circle.

Now for the *good* news!

YOU CAN STOP IT SPINNING!

You know the great thing about circles? They turn both ways!

In the same way that just one thing (an altered thought) led to everything else getting worse, you can start to make it better by changing one thing.

Just by acting differently, or changing the way you think about some things, you can affect all the other things in the circle and start to feel better.

Sounds too easy? Turn over for an example.

How to stop
the circle

Start here

1. You're walking down the street and someone you know ignores you

Oh no! She doesn't like me!

---

4. You have no energy and maybe can't sleep that night for worrying about what happened – altered physical symptoms

Oh no! She doesn't like me!

I feel down

What's wrong with me? I feel tired and exhausted

I don't want to see anyone at the moment

Now lets stop the circle!

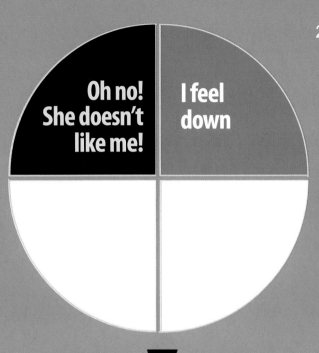

2. This makes you
feel bad —
altered feelings

3. You go home and
avoid other people's
company — altered
behaviour

21

Start here

1. You're walking down the street and someone you know ignores you

Poor Louise, she must be upset, I wonder what's wrong?

4. You arrange to see Louise later and discuss practical things you can do to help

Poor Louise, she must be upset, I wonder what's wrong?

Is there anything I can do?

I feel really great, alert and strong

I feel good about myself because I'm helping someone else

See how it works?

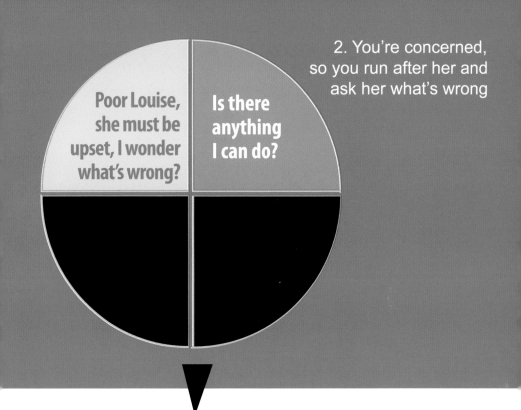

2. You're concerned, so you run after her and ask her what's wrong

3. Louise explains and you listen like a good friend

YOU
HAVE
CONTROL

You just need to change one thing

You can take control and stop the vicious circle by changing just one thing – your thinking, your response, your activities – almost anything. And it doesn't have to be a big thing!

You could start by changing the way you react. By going out just one time. By doing just a bit more exercise. By changing the way you think about things.

If you manage to do something about just one thing, you'll break the vicious circle, stop it spinning down and down and start to feel better straight away.

So here's what to do. Pick one small thing then use the Planner sheet on pages 26/27 to give yourself the best start.

Once you're done, use the Review sheet on pages 28/29 to check your progress.

Go, make a plan

DON'T JUST SIT THERE, MAKE A PLAN!

1. WHAT AM I GOING TO DO?

2. WHEN AM I GOING TO DO IT?

3. WHAT PROBLEMS OR DIFFICULTIES COULD ARISE, AND HOW CAN I OVERCOME THEM?

Is my planned task

Q. USEFUL FOR UNDERSTANDING OR CHANGING HOW I AM?

YES ☐ NO ☐

Q. SPECIFIC, SO THAT I WILL KNOW WHEN I HAVE DONE IT?

YES ☐ NO ☐

Q. REALISTIC, PRACTICAL AND ACHIEVABLE?

YES ☐ NO ☐

MY NOTES

OK, HOW DID IT GO?

WHAT DID YOU PLAN TO DO?
WRITE IT HERE

DID YOU TRY TO DO IT?

YES ☐ **NO** ☐

IF YES:
1. WHAT WENT WELL?

2. WHAT DIDN'T GO SO WELL?

3. WHAT HAVE YOU LEARNED FROM WHAT HAPPENED?

4. HOW ARE YOU GOING TO APPLY WHAT YOU HAVE LEARNED?

IF NO: WHAT STOPPED YOU?

INTERNAL THINGS
(FORGOT, TOO TIRED, PUT IT OFF, DIDN'T THINK I COULD DO IT, COULDN'T SEE THE POINT ETC.).

EXTERNAL THINGS
(OTHER PEOPLE, WORK OR HOME ISSUES ETC.).

HOW COULD YOU HAVE PLANNED TO TACKLE THESE THINGS?

Next steps...

Use the five areas vicious circle to make sense of why you feel the way you do. Remember, that's not all you've discovered. You've also learned some targets for change that will make a big difference.

What changes do you need to make in each of the five areas? When you've sorted your current problem, you might want to choose another little book and work on something else in your life.

You can get added help and support by working through the free linked online courses at www.llttf.com.

Go for it!